APPREHENDED *for* LIFE

by
Montez Bullock

Thanks so much Kim
your Spirit is sweet

Montez Bullock

MY FATHER'S BUSINESS PUBLICATIONS

Apprehended4Life@yahoo.com
(404) 447-5405

Published by My Father's Business Publications
P.O. Box 64
Atlanta, GA 30301
www.MontezBullock.com

Apprehended4Life@yahoo.com
(404) 447-5405

Unless otherwise noted, all Scripture quotations are taken from the *Holy Bible, New International Version*. *NIV*.

Copyright © 1973, 1978, 1984 by International Bible Society.
Used by permission of Zondervan Publishing House. All rights reserved.

Most names in this book have been changed to respect the privacy of the individuals.

Book Design: AuthorSupport.com

ISBN: 978-0-9883509-0-8

Printed in the United States of America

To Ma, who turned me over to God
and never stopped praying.

"Montez Bullock is a true testament of how God can take your trials and turn them into triumphs. This book will bless your life as you turn each page and read the story of a young man who dared to be different."

~ **BISHOP PAUL S. MORTON, SR.**
Changing A Generation Ministries, Senior Pastor, Atlanta, GA

TABLE OF CONTENTS

ACKNOWLEDGMENTS

I COULD NOT have written this book without the expert editing and publishing assistance of Michael J. Dowling (http://www.MichaelJDowling.com). Thank you, Mike, for your commitment to this effort. You truly served me "as working for the Lord" (Colossians 3:23).

I also want to extend my heartfelt appreciation to Jerry and Michelle Dorris of Author Support (http://www.AuthorSupport.com), who did a superb job of laying out the interior of this book and designing the cover. Thank you for going the extra mile on behalf of "one of the least of these" (Matthew 25:40).

PREFACE

I'VE SPENT MOST of the thirty-three years of my life running from the law. Lots of times I got away. Sometimes I was caught and let off, and more times than I can count I was apprehended and sent to jail or prison. I never killed anybody, but I did just about everything else.

In the end, though, there was one lawgiver I couldn't get away from. I spent my life running from him, but he pursued me until I finally surrendered. He apprehended me, but instead of imprisonment, he gave me freedom. He convicted me, but instead of punishment, he gave me forgiveness. He took away my lust for money and my craving for the happiness I never could seem to find, and he replaced them with immeasurable wealth and unspeakable joy. I deserved the death penalty, but he gave me eternal life.

The Bible tells me in Jeremiah 1:5 that God knew me before he formed me in my mother's womb. Jeremiah 29:11 says,

> *For I know the plans I have for you," declares the Lord, "plans to prosper you and not to harm you, plans to give you hope and a future.*

I wouldn't have believed those words when I was going in and out of group homes, hospitals, youth detention camps, jails, and prisons. I couldn't have imagined they were true when I was battling drug addictions and dodging gunshots and robbing stores and running from the cops. But God's plans were bigger and better than anything I could imagine, and his power is greater than the snares of the streets. Looking back I can see that he had his hand on me all along. As I was delivered from prison to prison, from danger to danger, no weapon formed against me prospered (Isaiah 54:17).

The Apostle Paul said, "Woe to me if I do not preach the gospel!" (1 Corinthians 9:16) I understand how he felt. I'm no Apostle Paul, but I am like him in this respect: I just have to tell people about the goodness of God. Jesus healed me and gave me new life. I'm so glad he apprehended me. I want to spend the rest of my life praising him. I'm compelled to tell people what Jesus did for me. That's why I'm writing this book.

I don't take any pride in authorship. As you will see when you read my story, I don't have anything to boast about. Jesus Christ deserves all the glory. I only want this book to glorify him. Paul said it perfectly in 1 Corinthians 1:26-31:

> *Brothers, think of what you were when you were called. Not many of you were wise by*

human standards; not many were influential, not many were of noble birth. But God chose the foolish things of the world to shame the wise; God chose the weak things of the world to shame the strong. He chose the lowly things of this world and the despised things — and the things that are not — to nullify the things that are, so that no one may boast before him. It is because of him that you are in Christ Jesus, who has become for us wisdom from God — that is, our righteousness, holiness and redemption. Therefore, as it is written, "Let him who boasts boast in the Lord."

Romans 8:28 really excites me. It says, "And we know that in all things God works for the good of those who love him, who have been called according to his purpose." I'm encouraged when I think about how God will somehow fulfill his good purposes from my sinful mistakes. My prayer is that he will employ even this simple book as part of his grander purpose for transforming lives. I pray that the Holy Spirit will use the words in these pages to captivate hearts and fill them with unspeakable joy.

CHAPTER 1

My Family

ON AUGUST 21, 1962, in Jackson, Mississippi, Caldonia Bullock, gave birth to my mother, Arlean (Bullock) Buckner, whom everyone calls "Lisa." Fifteen years later I was born into the same violent, poverty-stricken, dope-infested, prostitution-plagued neighborhood she grew up in. For some reason, everyone calls this area "The North End," even though it's in the center of downtown, only about four or five minutes away from the capitol building.

Grandma Cal raised a total of nine children. She died at age fifty-five after suffering a stroke, when I was about ten or eleven. I remember her cleaning up the kitchen and cooking, and at the same time talking and entertaining company, constantly on her swollen feet all day. She was on the "mother board" at the church, and she was all the time telling us to "STOP CHUNKIN DEM ROCKS FO YALL PUT SOMEBODY EYE OUT OR BUSS A WINDA!"

APPREHENDED *for* LIFE

My mother and her mom had a strange relationship. They were always fussing, cursing, yelling, and screaming. Grandma put my ma out of her house when she was fifteen years old and pregnant with me, but she showed her good side by paying Ma's first year's rent on her new place.

Life was always a struggle, especially after that first year, because our income was so low. Ma would spend her entire welfare check on rent and still be a couple of dollars short. I was little, but I remember being sent out to neighbors and being taken to food pantries and anyplace else Ma could think of where we might get something to eat.

My biological father was hardly in my life. My stepdad, Chauncey, whom I sometimes call "Pop," started dating Ma when I was only nine months old. They married and have been together since. He's nine years older than Ma, born one day before her, and from the same neighborhood. He was a hustler of cocaine and other drugs, and sometimes he used them. He always was a hard worker, as far as I can recall. Even though he seemed to love the streets, he kept doing his job. Sometimes—actually lots of times—he would work Monday through Friday, come home, give Ma her money, and we wouldn't see him until Sunday night or Monday morning, when he headed back to work.

He'd leave the money on the dresser. When Ma came

home, if that money wasn't there, she would fly out the door with my sister and me in tow, looking for Chauncey with a flashlight in the daylight. We would go hunting for Chauncey down streets, in clubs, in houses and apartments, you name it.

Chauncey is the father of my sister, Chacey Shivell Buckner, born on October 15, 1983, five years after me. She always had a sweet spirit, which is kind of unique in our family. We grew up with six uncles and two aunts on our mom's side of the family, and something was always going on.

Ma was diagnosed with paranoid schizophrenia when she was nineteen and had to stay at the state hospital. Maybe that's one reason why she and her ma (my grandma) argued all the time. Ma's sisters and brothers didn't like their arguing and broke off the relationship with Ma at times. But Ma always wanted them to just accept her. She wanted to feel loved, that's all. Unfortunately, she still desires that now, even though she doesn't force her love on them anymore.

Even today, when a family member gets locked up or needs a place to stay, sometimes Ma is the first one to get called, and she's always ready to help. Just recently one of her twin brothers, my Uncle Ed, was hospitalized. His health started failing badly while he was in prison. After he was released, his feet started swelling. He lost his kidneys and went on dialysis. Afterwards, he started drinking, fell, and almost broke his neck. I found out while he was in the hospital that he had fluid on his spinal cord, and that he could hardly move. This was an uncle who never wanted much to do with Ma because he didn't want to hear her talk about God. Ma offered to bring him to her house to take care of him, in spite of what he had said and done to her over the years.

My mom and her sisters and brothers have had hard lives. Here are some details of how my siblings are living today.

My Uncle Frank fell out a tree and broke his neck while doing landscaping work a couple of years ago. His own twin brother, Uncle Ed, watched it happen.

Uncle Jay, another uncle who had been smoking crack since I can remember, was shot seven times in one leg by a rifle while walking home late one night. He has problems with his pancreas from drinking.

Uncle C.J. served a nine-year prison sentence for manslaughter. He always loved to drink, and that made him violent. He was in the same state prison in Mississippi as his sixteen-year-old son, who was serving time for armed robbery.

Uncle Flint, the oldest of Ma's brothers, did the best.

He went to college, got a degree in electrical engineering, and worked on airplanes in Wichita, Kansas. Later, after Grandma Cal died, he moved back home and got strung out on crack cocaine. After years of battling with the addiction, he finally recovered and moved back to Kansas and found a decent job. Recently, he had a heart attack. Uncle Ed sold crack in Grandma's house, and the once well-kempt home turned into a dope house where neighborhood crack smokers hung out. Even the drug dealers hung out there. So did I.

Uncle Peanut, the youngest of all of Ma's brothers and sisters, also smokes crack cocaine.

Not long ago, Aunt Mary's son, Javoris, died at age ten of a gunshot wound to the head. I visited him in the hospital and saw him lying in the bed with a hole in his head. Aunt Mary is still taking it hard.

Aunt Rachel, the second oldest of Grandma Caldonia's children, was strung out on crack cocaine as long as I knew her. She suffered from AIDS and was always going in and out of the hospital. She's dead now, may she rest in peace.

Those are my aunts and uncles I grew up around, my family who I love dearly on Mom's side. On my dad's side of the family, his mom, Renae, who I also call Ma, had three sons.

My dad, whom they call "Big Mack," was the oldest.

He and his dad stayed drunk all the time. He developed kidney problems and ended up on dialysis. About a year ago he was blessed with a kidney transplant, but he started back drinking again.

I look a lot like my dad. When I saw a picture of him when he was about twenty years old, I seriously thought it was a picture of me, until I noticed he was wearing the different fashion of that time. Mom told me that my dad went into the army when I was one year old. He didn't come to see her when she was in the hospital giving birth to me, so she changed my name because she didn't want me to be identified with him.

I was an important part of my parent's lives at first, but then dad was hardly ever around. We never really spent time together as father and son, even though I wanted it. I eventually got used to it, though. They said he played basketball pretty well, but he never saw me hoop, and that hurt me coming up. I always tried to have a relationship with him, but I ended up giving up the effort.

Roger Mack, Sr, who was known by everyone as "Shark," died in 2009 of pancreatic cancer. Like my dad, he used to get drunk every day of the week with his dad, my grandpa. He once went to prison for seven years. He scared me many times, warning me as a child about prison. He had a way of speaking to me, looking serious as can be.

He tried his best to let me know about the other side and how tough it is.

The third brother was Uncle Theodore Mack. He is the most productive man in my family. He was my father figure and still is today. I just got rebellious and let him down. We have since talked, and I'm thankful he's forgiven me.

CHAPTER 2

My Home

WE LIVED IN a small house at 206 Roosevelt Street in Jackson, Mississippi. It had only one bedroom, so we also had beds in the living room. Across the street was a club called "Sonny's," where the whole neighborhood seemed to hang out. It was so close to our house that you could easily hear the blues playing and the loud talking all hours of the day and night. They were always partying at Sonny's and at another club right by our house. My cousin Lil Jay lived close by, too. His dad sold dope out of his house, may he rest in peace.

People would walk beside our house constantly to take a shortcut to the next street, smoke crack, and hide from police. All kinds of stuff went on in that little alleyway. We had absolutely no privacy. Many times people would tease me, saying that they heard my mom giving me a whipping. Those thin walls at the house would allow you to hear a pin drop.

I remember those whippings! The extension cords, which felt like they would go straight through me, left marks shaped like a funny letter "C." I would run all over the house, and that only made it worse. But who is going to sit there and take it?

Ma kept that little house cleaner than the state board of health. She cleaned a lot, but somehow we kept roaches. I remember as a youngster running to the bathtub and turning on the lights to see how many roaches would be in the tub. There were so many that it was hard to see what color the tub was. They were all over, even in the kitchen. When you would turn the lights on, they scattered everywhere, like when you stir up an ant bed.

I really can't see why so many roaches were interested in our house, because food was scarce. I remember so well eating rice and lunchmeat every day. Mom cooks pretty good now, but back then she was still learning. The rice was more like mashed potatoes, but thank God she did feed me.

When I say I fell asleep at the table every time I ate, I really and truly mean it. Ma literally made me eat my food till I could not eat any more. She made sure I was full and not just playing with food. After she had fed me, she would go to the house of a lady in the neighborhood for her own meal. This other person wasn't clean at all, and Ma was making a sacrifice for me.

My Home

I remember one day like it was last week. I was maybe seven or eight. Hart, the dad of one of my cousins, was holding a big chrome handgun to the head of another of my cousins named Cool, who was close to my dad's age. Looking back, I figure it was probably a 357 revolver with a six-inch barrel. Cool was on his knees. I told Ma, and she ran Hart off from our back yard. Our house was right in a pathway that the entire neighborhood walked through, so this kind of stuff happened a lot.

Mom had to go eat at other places because she and her ma, her sisters, and her brothers hardly got along at all. One day we were in bed with Ma, and a guy burst in the house with a gun, grabbed my Ma, and shot the ceiling. One bullet almost hit me, my mom, and my sister. Every time after that, whenever I looked at the ceiling, I would remember we could have gotten killed.

One day Chauncey was at home asleep in the bed, while I was getting myself ready for school. The day before, one of my classmates had been showing off some cologne at school, so I decided to do the same thing. While Ma was still in bed, I went to the bathroom and put the Polo, Safari, Chaps, and other colognes in my pocket.

I didn't know at the time that she knew I had all those cologne bottles in my pocket. She let me go all the way to school without saying a word. Later that day, she popped

11

up at Brown Elementary, asked my teacher for her paddle, and wore me out right there.

Another day I stole her money off of the dresser. Ma realized it by the time I was at school. Yep, she tore me up and didn't care who saw it—Ma didn't care at all.

I thought Ma was way too strict. She always was ready to wear me out, but she never played with me. Looking back, though, I'm glad she was strict, because if she had been too lenient, I would probably be dead now.

I was pretty tough. I went to school early in the morning to help the kitchen workers set up the food and beverages. While doing that, I would slip off to my classroom and steal writing utensils and change grades in the grade book, because nobody was at school that early except the kitchen workers and me. Even though I changed my grades, I didn't need to that much. I did fairly well in elementary school, especially considering I didn't have anyone to help me with my work. Ma didn't have any education, so she couldn't do anything but make me do my homework and behave.

CHAPTER 3

Fun and Games

I HAD A cousin named Cory, whom we called "Little C.J.," or just "C.J." Growing up, we were like real brothers. C.J. was the son of Uncle C.J., my mother's brother. We would compete on our tests at school all the time. It was fun to be in class with my best friend, first cousin, and brother. We loved to "flip." That's what we called it. We would go to different neighborhoods and do gymnastics in the middle of the street, off of cars, and on the grass. We'd also compete in street tournaments.

My mom never could afford to put me in gymnastics classes, but C.J. and I learned on our own. I was pretty good, they said, and C.J. was even better. We could do a backward flip with a complete 360 degree twist before landing on the ground. When we had mats, they were simply filthy old mattresses that looked like they had housed stray dogs for years. Some were little more than rusty springs, but we still would stack them on top of each other and flip on them all day long. We loved it.

Basketball was big to us, too. We played at the parks, but mostly we shot ball behind someone's house. Instead of a regular goal, we used a bicycle rim nailed on a tree. We had to make our own place to play, because the older guys hooped at the public park. We'd wear out the grass, so we'd have to play in the dirt. When I went home, my socks, shirt, and hair would be full of dirt.

We played tag football in the middle of the street. When cars came, we'd just get on the side until they passed on by. We played tackle football in the grass with no equipment. We picked rocks up in buckets and chucked them at each other until the first person got hurt. We were rough, but it was normal to us.

My cousin C.J. was a great fighter, and most of our peers couldn't beat him. I was one of the few who would fight him. We would fight, and then we'd cry and make up. We did this just about every day. If we didn't fight each other, we fought somebody else. Our older cousins, G-Man and Doughboy, would urge us on. I don't know what we really liked the most—basketball, flipping, or fighting—because we seemed to constantly be doing all three.

G-Man and Doughboy were the younger sons of Aunt Rachel, my mom's older sister. They did whatever they wanted, because their mom treated them as if they were her friends. She didn't seem to care that they called her Rachel and cursed around her and to her. Ma would probably have killed me if someone had told her I cursed.

C.J. and I hung out together most of our youth, and there was something that happened to both of us that is hard to talk about, even now. A man in the neighborhood sexually molested us. I don't remember how old we were, but we were very young. That incident really brought us down. We wondered why that had to happen to us. It made us angry, and a lot of the acting out we did later was because of that. People thought we were just bad, but deep down we felt sad, disappointed, and let down, like no one understood us but us. Plus, I felt I was less fortunate than others. That is why we got in so much trouble.

Bad things were happening all the time. That same guy later molested some other kids in the neighborhood. After I was grown, he went to jail for raping a girl, but he got out quick—too quick.

One day when I was around eleven or twelve, Doughboy's best friend shot the brains out of a guy in a car while Doughboy and C.J. were in it. Doughboy was maybe fourteen or fifteen at the time, and C.J. was about twelve. They said the guy's brain was coming out of his head.

When Doughboy was about fifteen, he started smoking crack cocaine, along with his brother G-Man. G-Man was about seventeen. The two of them and their older brother Donny, whom we called Don-Don, regularly used to get high with their ma, Aunt Rachel. Don-Don has spent half of his life, if not most of his life, going in and out of jail.

I once saw a gun on the dresser in my Uncle Peanut's room in Grandma Caldonia's house, and I told C.J. about it. The next thing I remember seeing was C.J. running back to the house with blood all over his T-shirt. Not long after that, a detective picked him up, but he later brought him back. It turned out that one of our friends had killed another friend with that gun. I'm thankful I wasn't there when it happened. It could have been me.

CHAPTER 4

Go West, Young Man

WHEN I WAS eleven, Uncle Theodore invited me to spend the summer with him in Seattle. My flight made stops in Dallas/Ft. Worth and Salt Lake City, where I stole souvenirs from the airport gift shops. In Seattle, Uncle Theodore picked me up and drove me to where he lived in Edmonds, Washington, right by the Pacific Ocean at Puget Sound. It was within walking distance of the beach and in sight of Mt. Rainer and Canada's Blue Mountains. That was the first time I had ever seen real mountains. His neighborhood was a big change from the police sirens, cursing, gun shots, and smells of Jackson. Uncle showed me his check stub. He was earning $19.25 per hour as a mechanical engineer, which back in 1989 seemed like mighty good pay to this kid.

Uncle Theodore's in-laws at the time, Mr. Tom and Miss Alice, treated me as if I were their own flesh and blood. They let me drive a car for the first time ever (they had a Mercedes Benz!), and they cruised me around in their red Porsche. Miss Alice, with her dreadlocks hanging down, rode me in their low-rider truck, too. It was strange to see a tall black woman with a white man. Mr. Tom was a short thick Caucasian, maybe even Italian, and they poured out their love on Montez. I remember going on Mr. Tom's yacht. It was the first time I ever saw something like that, a real home on water.

Aunt Sally, Uncle Theodore's first wife, invited me to spend three weeks with her in Portland, Oregon. I remember riding with her in her new BMW up a tall hill, where she lived with a man who played professional basketball for the Seattle Supersonics. We even went shopping at a Nike factory. This exposure to successful people made me want a better life. I'd had enough of killers and drug dealers.

After she brought me back from the fun we had, I ended up finding a job at a flower shop cutting flowers. My take averaged around $10 a day. But I still had too much mischief in me for my own good. One day, while Uncle Theodore was at work, I took a walk with his dog and shoplifted an outfit for my sister. I ran out of the store with the dog in one hand and the clothes in the other. I was so nervous that I got lost. The police caught me and took me and the dog to the precinct. I begged them not to put me in jail, because I didn't want my Uncle Theodore to find out what I'd done. They finally agreed to let me wash the fire trucks as compensation, which I did. Uncle Theodore found out anyway. I honestly can't remember what he did, but he probably knocked me out.

To make matters worse, Delta Airlines called the house and told Uncle Theodore that I had stolen from airport shops. They'd captured it all on their security cameras. Uncle Theodore spanked me on my butt and tore me up. He once tried out for the Dallas Cowboys, so he was no weakling.

In spite of my acting out, Uncle Theodore asked my mom if he could keep me there with him, but Ma said no. After three months, she wanted me home. I will always be grateful for his generosity and for what he taught me. I learned to open doors for women, to not slur when I speak, and things like that. He inspired me to want a better life and to be productive.

CHAPTER 5

On the Move

WHEN I RETURNED home to Jackson, I was surprised to find my little sister, Chacey, dressed in a hospital gown with a bandage on her head. She had fallen out of a buggy and fractured her skull. The government gave mom financial assistance, which helped us as a family for a while, but one day it abruptly stopped.

A short time later, we moved about five minutes away to 136 East Church Street in downtown Jackson. It was a duplex and larger than our old place, but in a worse neighborhood. In fact, to this day they call that neighborhood "The Dungeon." There was a park in our back yard where prostitutes took their customers and just about everything else happened that you could imagine. Our neighbors on both sides of the duplex dealt drugs. A man got beat up in front of our house, and I believe he died. People were getting shot; I got pursued by the prostitutes; it was terrible. One day Ma, my sister, and I came home to find bullet holes in the front wall and door.

I shined shoes at John's Barber Shop around the corner on Farish Street in the historic district, where I made $40 to $60 a week. I was only twelve, but the working girls, as we called them, would try to solicit me. They didn't care; money was money.

Ma would send my sister and me to church, where I was a junior deacon. I'll never forget reading the scriptures every Sunday before the congregation. I slept most of the time the reverend was preaching. Robert Creamer and I sat together with the older deacons. Our grandmothers were best friends, and we had played together since we were toddlers. Robert died of AIDS not long ago.

During those childhood days, I wrote Billy Graham, and he sent me prayer cloths. My buddy Jack Fields would come to our house to witness about God. Today he is serving ninety-nine years for robbery and murder. He also killed his cellmate in the county jail.

Sometimes on Saturdays, Ma would let me go play. C.J. and our other friends would come get me. One particular Saturday, C.J. had a stolen gun that belonged to his girlfriend's dad. A bunch of us, all around the age of twelve, walked a long way to a guy's house. C. J. fired the gun at the house, and then we all took off running. Nobody got caught for that one, though.

We would always be doing a lot of crazy stuff with that gun, until one day C.J. pulled it out in class. I figured we might get into trouble, so I asked the teacher for a restroom pass, and put the gun in my locker. A short time later they called C.J. and me to the office. He went downtown to the police precinct and told the people at the school where the gun was. I got busted, too. I was more scared of Ma finding out than anything else. For less serious offenses, she would come after me with a whole tree branch as a switch. No telling what she would do to me for playing with a gun!

They expelled C.J. for the rest of the year. They only "sentenced" me to twenty days at the alternative school, where the kids did pretty much as they pleased—sort of like the movie *Lean on Me*, only much smaller. Ma took care of me, though. She paddled me so hard and so long that it nearly worn out the principal's paddle. At least that paddling got me off with twenty days of suspension instead of expulsion.

Ma constantly chastised me throughout my life. She wouldn't ever let me have a hole in my ear or go around with my shirt hanging out of my pants or my jeans sagging. I had to say "yes sir" or "yes ma'am," instead of "yeah," and I couldn't stay out past dark like most of my peers got to do.

Despite the trouble I got into with the gun, I won a spot on the student body council as the secretary of the school. Also, I was voted "Mr. 7th Grader." The office secretary told me that if they had not eliminated the "best dressed" category, I would have won that, too. She meant that as a sincere compliment. Ma had taught me how to coordinate my clothes and iron them as good as the cleaners would do. I would iron everything she washed for me as soon as she brought them home from the Laundromat. I hated doing that ironing at the time, but it taught me to be clean and responsible. As I got older, I realized the value of what she taught me and loved her for it. To this day, I like to dress well and coordinate the colors of my clothes.

CHAPTER 6

On the Move Again...and Again

OUR DUPLEX CAUGHT fire in 1992, when I was in the 8th grade, and we lost just about everything we had. God spared our lives, and three weeks later we had a better house with better furniture in a better neighborhood. Saint Andrew's Church in downtown Jackson helped us tremendously and gave us furniture, which Ma still has today. I ended up staying with Grandma Renae, who bought me lots of outfits to replace the clothes I had lost. Thanks to the fire, I had all of the latest fashions, including the newest shoes.

You may remember that I told you that when my sister fractured her skull, the government was sending us payments, but after a while the checks abruptly stopped. It turned out the government had made a mistake. Not long after our house burned down, Ma got a surprise call: we were owed about $30,000 in back payments. She used that money to buy a new house in a neighborhood away from the drugs, prostitution, and violence. She put us in a Christian private school and bought two used vehicles.

Ma told me that when she was about twenty years old, she used to lie on her bed thinking about a three-bedroom home for her family. She said that God had given her the desires of her heart, and to top it off, my sister's head had completely healed and she no longer had to have special education or medicine. I believe God allowed all of these things to happen just to bless us!

I was a teenager now, and my head was getting harder by the day. I was playing football for Rowan Middle School. I also played tennis, because Ma said my Uncle Theodore had played it and was good. I played a bit of soccer, too, but basketball gave me the most joy. I played at the same school my dad had played for and even wore the exact number as he did. Even though he wasn't in my life, I admired my dad and desired to be his friend.

There were a number of great players on the basketball team, so I didn't start, but I was the first guy off the bench, the sixth man. That year I earned awards for best defensive player, best free throw shooter, and most improved player. One home game, I stole the ball five or six times in rapid succession, scoring on some of those steals. The crowd went wild cheering my name. I would have given anything for my dad to have been there to support me, but he never came, no matter how many times I asked him.

In the summer before high school, I started attending a teen center called Tiffany's. It was named after a girl who died from electrocution while talking on a phone in the bathtub. At the club, I met a girl and we got sexually involved. I stayed away from home for weeks at a time. Ma said I began to "smell myself," which meant that I had become very rebellious and full of myself. I loved being free. I stayed at my girlfriend's house, slept in her bed, and rode with her in her car. I felt grown.

After about nine months we moved again to an even better house. I was rebellious and prideful and got into lots of mischief. Ma told me what was right, but I just got caught up in the streets. That 8th-grade summer I changed dramatically. Anytime Ma tried to discipline me or talk to me about what I was doing, I ran away from home.

I'd run to my girlfriend's house, where I had freedom. She sold cocaine and was popular around a lot of people. She had her own car and money, so I was just loose in the streets. I would stay away from home for three weeks at a time. From 1992 to 1997, the longest I stayed home was around three months. If I wasn't at my girlfriend's, I was on the streets or mostly in jail. I was locked up 60 to 70 times for drugs, burglary, auto theft, gun charges, or just running away. The people at the youth court detention center thought I should have counseling, so I went to hospitals out of town. They sent me to the Our House (a group home) and the Crisis Center in Jackson. I was sent to boot camp twice at Oakley and at Columbia Training Schools. I ran away from Oakley and from the youth detention center, but I got caught both times.

All my life, Ma would stay on me, and I would just go the other direction. I had a favorite phrase: "I don't care." I said that about everything. I was headed down the wrong road at a fast pace.

I envied the dope boys riding around with the girls in their fancy cars, all painted up with the shiny rims. I wanted the money, fame, and the respect they had on the street. I was going the wrong way in an attempt to make it happen. At age fourteen, I was into robberies, car jackings (taking cars by force of a gun), car thefts, and selling crack cocaine. We stayed away from authority and did what we wanted to do. All the while I'd hear in my head the teachings Ma used to try to drill into me:

"Trouble is easy to get into, but hard to get out of."

"Don't go to prison, because it's going to be hard to get me to come visit you."

"A disobedient child shall never live the number of their days."

One day, while four of us were stealing cars, I got a

gun out of a car we had stolen. I went to the mall and ran out of a clothing store with seven outfits. We had already planned to go on a robbing spree, and I didn't intend to go back home anytime soon; that's why I needed the clothes. As we attempted to get away, the car we had stolen got a flat tire. We tried to break into several more cars in other parking lots, but something always interfered, so we fled those areas on foot, leaving a long crime trail behind.

As we were walking along Lynch Street, in front of a bowling alley, a car blocked all four of us. Two of the guys I was with ran across the street. I ran the other way with the third guy, but he split from me. Suddenly I noticed a man with a gun chasing me. He was yelling, "Get down! Get down! Get down!" I pointed my gun back at him and continued to run. Then I had a strong feeling to stop running, so I fell down. He snatched me up, dragged me over to the side of a building, and said, "I was just about to shoot you. I'm tired of people like you breaking in people's stuff. I'm going to kill you right here!" I was on my knees in the dark, crying out to the Lord for help.

Then this guy revealed his identity; he was a cop. He told me he could have shot me and just worked his pen on the paperwork. A short time later TV and newspaper reporters were there, but we were too young to have our identities revealed in the media. I was only fifteen, and I knew I'd be going to boot camp. But that day I was glad, because it beat getting killed.

Between the ages of fourteen and seventeen, I stole cars, robbed jewelry stores, stole clothing, sold drugs, and even tried to rob the customers of prostitutes. I got shot at and went to jail many times. When I reached a certain age, my name and photo began appearing on local television as one of the area's most wanted criminals. I was a stupid fool on an involuntary suicide mission, blind as a bat but not able to see. Many of the friends I had back then have gotten themselves killed or have been sentenced to life in prison. I thank God for sparing me.

CHAPTER 7

Called

I WOULD GO to my grandma's house sometimes when I wanted to get away from my ma. One day sweet Grandma had had enough, and she put me out of her house. I left, but I ended up breaking back in, stealing her belongings and my cousin's stuff. I know that I was a no-good rat, stealing from my grandma. She forgave me, but I felt so bad because I loved Renae Mack, and still do.

By now I was eighteen years old, and things just kept getting worse. I got caught breaking into a house looking for drugs to sell. As the police were booking me at the precinct, I ran to the barber shop across the street. They caught me again and beat me up pretty bad. Then they sent me to the county jail.

I started fasting and praying, like I'd been taught in church when I was fourteen. I read the Bible and confessed to a cellmate something that occurred in my past that I had kept secret. The Lord then opened the doors of the county jail after I had been there eleven days.

I went home that night looking for the guns I had hid. I couldn't find them—I learned later that my mom had thrown them away—but I did get the marijuana my stepdad had put up for me. I left to go get a haircut, but wound up getting high instead. I was right back at the same place again. It seemed I could never get my life straight.

As I headed home, I started thinking of the scriptures I had read in jail. The trees were blowing and I thought about how Proverbs 30: 4 says that God gathers the wind in his fists. Normally, I would have left any desire to read the Bible back in jail, but not this time. I walked in the house, locked myself in my room, and got on my knees with a Bible. Then I did something my mother had always said to do—I asked God for understanding before I started reading. I opened the Word up to a random page. It turned out to be a verse in Proverbs that talked about how a fool is hardheaded and doesn't listen.

Never in my life had I ever experienced anything like this. It seemed that God was talking directly to me. Some of the things I was guilty of flashed before me in my mind, especially about Ma's teachings that I had always rejected. I started shaking and crying. I pleaded with God to give me another chance and to not allow me to die. The conviction, distress, and anguish were overwhelming.

It was a powerful, dreadful, fearful encounter with the Creator. I never understood the King James Version until that day. God opened my mind to understand his Word. I felt he was speaking to me directly using an internal audible voice.

As the intensity of this supernatural experience eased off just a little bit, God guided me back to the Word. I felt that my life was over, and that I was without any hope. I had experienced the fear of a gun to my head, so I knew how it felt to think that I was about to die. But this fear was way more intense, because it was a supernatural revelation from the Spirit of God.

I picked up the Bible again and kept reading. My eyes landed on the 33rd verse of the first chapter of Proverbs: "But whoever listens to me will live in safety and be at ease, without fear or harm." As I read those words, I had a powerful supernatural experience. My fears were instantly taken away, and I had an overwhelming awareness of God's grace and love and compassion for me. I felt so much peace.

I immediately ran into the hall where I met Ma. I screamed, "Ma! Ma! I am sorry for all of the wrong that I said or did to you!" That was the day the Lord called me: February 26, 1997. I was 18 years old.

CHAPTER 8

Lost

AFTER I RECONCILED with Ma, it seemed like it would take forever for Friday to come when we'd get to go to church. When I finally got there, I took the microphone and gave God the glory in my testimony. I talked about my past ways of life and how God had called me. I had heard of supernatural things happening to people over the years, but I had never expected or imagined something like that would happen to me. Some cases I heard about seemed too "super" to believe. But what happened to me was real. God in his grace had given me another chance at life. He delivered me from ALL of my sins that I had committed, even in my thoughts. I had fought them hard, but I had never been able to get free of them. Only he could set me free!

I was on fire for God. The word was getting around that Montez Bullock had changed. I was serving Jehovah now. Even though I was praising God and testifying about what he had done for me, the enemy kept assaulting me. Different women would pursue me. I knew that the Bible says that a Christian should not be unequally yoked; that is, he shouldn't be married to someone who is not a believer. The devil couldn't get at me outside the church, so he tried another tactic. He tempted me inside the church. I can't put all the fault on the devil, though. I deserve a lot of the blame.

After a while I started slacking off in my prayer life. When I was prayed up, I noticed I was stronger than when my prayer life was less active. Before, I would have bypassed temptation. But now, since I wasn't as prayerful, my mind started to drift. Finally, lust got stronger, and I gave in.

My eyes landed on a woman at church who was praising God. I figured this was my chance to get the desires of my heart. After all, I was close to eighteen months without being with a woman sexually. There were people in my life who were concerned about my hanging out with this woman. Out of concern, they went to the pastor, but I ignored all the warnings.

Even though I considered the pastor to be my teacher, mentor, and godfather, I wouldn't let his warnings get through to me. I couldn't see what he meant when he said this woman was not good for me. I kept thinking about Proverbs 18:22, which says, "He who finds a wife finds what is good and receives favor from the LORD." I was blind and actually thought that this woman was my opportunity to be obedient, which would then get me rewarded by God. I got tired of being told this woman wasn't for me, so I left my mom's house. A buddy God had placed in my life was living with my mom. He was a good friend, but I left him, too.

I went to stay with my dad's ma, Ms. Renae. There I could have more room and be comfortable doing what I wanted to do. This woman was maybe twelve or thirteen years older than me. One thing that kept me interested in her was that people thought we were having sex, but we were not even touching or kissing. I felt that gossip wasn't right. Three months later, we began to touch each other; then touching turned into kissing, and one day we had sex.

After we had sex, I felt like I had died, which I had done spiritually. Satan began to play with my thoughts and accuse me. I felt so guilty. As I waddled in my mess, I started feeling out of place in church. Before I had sat on the front row, where I would be encouraging the preacher, experiencing the anointing of God through the message, and testifying. Now I started sitting further and further back, until very shortly I was out the door. I eventually left this woman, because I felt she was the reason I had fallen away from God. She tried to pursue me, but I wasn't interested. I felt lost and confused. My disobedience had created a big void inside me.

CHAPTER 9

Jail

AT THAT TIME I had a job at the state hospital, but I lost it. Later, my mom, who was pregnant with my brother, was admitted to the same hospital. She had stopped taking her psychiatric medicine. She was afraid it would cause the baby she was carrying to be born retarded. Thanks to the Lord and Ma's carefulness, when my brother, Chauncey Solomon Buckner, was born, he was perfectly healthy.

I started back smoking cigarettes, drinking, chasing girls, and doing all the things I had done before. I even got into the hardcore street life, robberies, and thefts, until my life really began to crumble. After about a year, I was worse off than ever before. Luke 11:24-26 talks about how when the evil spirits are cleaned out of a house, the house must be kept clean or seven new spirits, more wicked than the first, will come in. That's what happened to me for the next thirteen paranoid years.

A voice inside me kept saying, "STOP THIS! LEAVE HERE! STOP HANGING WITH THEM! GO TO CHURCH! DO RIGHT!" My deepest desire was to be back in God, but I wasn't strong enough. I remembered the peace I had had in him, and I wanted it back. Nothing was like that clean, clear conscience I once had. I missed it, but I was so wrapped up in sin I couldn't get free. Satan had me pinned down and bound. I was so blind I couldn't see my way back.

One year later after I fornicated and chose to fall from Bible teachings and the teachings of my elders, I was back full force hustling in the streets. I did whatever I was able to do to fulfill my fleshly desires. I'm so grateful that God's grace and what I learned in the eighteen months I had walked with God kept me from dropping completely off the cliff. I knew God was protecting me when I couldn't do certain bad things I wanted to do, like dealing drugs. I couldn't do some things, because of the fear I had experienced the day God called me. I think that was God protecting me from some worse dangers.

One day I decided to sell crack cocaine anyway, in spite of my vow to stay away from it. I got caught and went to jail. Out on bond, I started selling fake watches, digital cameras, I-pods, and necklaces with real price tags in what looked like original boxes. This seemed to be an easier way to make money than selling drugs. It wasn't a felony, and I didn't have to be on the streets with the killers and robbers. But I could never prosper like I tried to. I felt that I was using the gift God gave me with the wrong motive in the wrong field.

I ended up back in jail anyway, and they wouldn't let me bond out this time. In the Hinds County Jail it was tough. I was in and out of isolation/maximum security (locked-down) cells. I had been around much danger on the streets, and I could always run away, but in jail you can't get away from the gangs.

Almost everyone I knew on the streets was in a gang, and I actually thought I was a member, because I always hung out with them and did everything they did. But when the gang leaders told me I would have to swear to certain things, I chose not to get more involved. They bullied me to purchase something off of the canteen sheet, which I refused to do. There was a price to pay. An assault left me with purple, red, and blue knots on my body.

I was sentenced to eighteen months and did about fifteen months total before I went home. I was only nineteen when I went to prison for the first time, but that was old compared to my cousin and friends I grew up with. When

I finally was released, Ma threw a "prodigal son" party with some members of the church at the house. Chauncey, my stepdad, fried the fish. To God be the glory, by this time the Lord had delivered him from crack cocaine, and he was a deacon in the church. Ma had faith that God would save me, too.

Unfortunately, I was hungrier now for money than at first. In fact, I felt I had to make up for lost time. I went to Chicago and started back selling the fake stuff. I went to jail for something I didn't do, but they let me out. I got involved with gangs, which in Chicago is much more dangerous. I met the wrong guys with guns, and I was headed down the wrong path. I think I would have been killed if I had stayed, but I decided to go back to Mississippi.

CHAPTER 10

Familiar Territory

AS SOON AS I got back to Jackson, I went on a crime spree. I took a big wad of $100 bills and a gold Rolex watch with at least 140 diamonds in it, and I spent all the money in about two days. I was moving fast in all kinds of crimes. Later, I got caught in a pawn shop with a very expensive ring. The police picked up a couple of other people with me. I was about to try to jump out of the window when one of them said he was guilty and that I hadn't been involved with this certain robbery, so they released me.

But I was picked up a week later and locked up. I thought I was going back to prison, but I was released from jail in three months and put on one-year probation. I was glad to be able to go home, but I still didn't acknowledge God. I was too caught up in the money and other allures of the world.

Back to selling drugs again, I went from this hustle to that hustle, whatever was convenient at the time. I spent my last dollar on buying some powder cocaine from a guy, because this offered the best chance to make some good money. I took the product to my side of town to get it cooked into crack. When it was cooked, not only was it short, but the quality wasn't what it was supposed to be.

I was upset and headed back to find the guy who sold me the bad drugs. While driving in the drizzling rain with partly cooked cocaine in a boiler in my lap, I ran into the vehicle in front of me, but I kept going because I had drugs in my lap.

When I arrived back at the guy's house, no one answered the door, so I drove away. As I sped along, the hood of my car flew off in the wind. I had owned the car for less than four months, but I had to sell it to get some quick money.

I was still desperate for cash, and now I had no vehicle and my name and face were on the local TV news station for the city's "most wanted" for another crime I had committed. I bought more drugs from another guy, and I found out later that the amount he gave me was less than I had paid for. I kept calling the guy who had cheated me, until I finally got in touch with him. He denied over and over again that he had shorted me. Talk wasn't getting me anywhere, so I changed my tactics and told him that I wanted to buy some more cocaine.

He met me where we had agreed, and I got in the back seat of his SUV. He and another guy were in the front seat. When he gave me the bag of cocaine, which was worth about $1,500 wholesale (that amount of good quality cocaine cooked would have retailed on the streets for about $4,500), I jumped out of the car and started running. This was my way of getting even and getting back the money I felt I was cheated out of.

I called one of my cousins and sold him the crack for far below wholesale price, just to get rid of it. Then I hid out in a hotel. After one or two months, I got a bus ticket from Jackson to Atlanta. It was September 11, 2001. I kept the other half of my roundtrip bus ticket in my pocket, just in case the security people at Greyhound asked to check it while looking for loiters. I was aware that they checked, because I used to hang out there at times.

I had only $320 with no change of clothes, and I knew very little about where I was. All I knew was that I was several hundred miles away from the police who were looking for me and from the enemies I had made in the streets of Jackson, so I had no plans to go back anytime soon.

But after a few months, I went back home, got a hotel room under a fictitious name, and entertained three women. I called an old buddy of mine to join me, and he brought over a guy, who happened to be the brother of one of the guys whose drugs I had taken. We were getting high on marijuana, and I noticed as I moved closer to this guy, he pulled his gun closer to himself on the bed. I moved closer again to see if he would react the same way, and he did. Something was wrong.

It was normal being around people you may have harmed; that's how it was in the streets. But this guy was very close to the enemies I had made, so I put everyone out, girls and all. As the guys drove off, the girls and I walked up front to the lobby. Standing there at the front counter was the guy who been in that SUV that day; he was the one who had actually put the drugs in my hand. I put two and two together and figured that he was asking the room clerk what room I was staying in. If I had registered using my real name, I probably wouldn't be here today.

I looked him in the eye and kept walking with the girls. Police security was there, so he didn't do anything. I walked out of the side door and noticed one of this guy's buddies driving off in a vehicle. At first I didn't notice another vehicle with more of this guy's buddies near the main doorway. When I did, I put my hand in my coat pocket as if I had a gun, looked him right in the eye, and got out of there.

CHAPTER 11

Atlanta

I WENT BACK to Atlanta, glad to be away from where I was a most wanted fugitive and from guys in the streets who were looking for revenge. Hard times had just begun, though. Often I had to steal food to eat. I was homeless, so I would go to the top floor of the Hilton, Crown Plaza, Hyatt Regency, and other hotels and check every door until I found one that was open. The first thing I would do was take a bath. If they ran me out, at least I would be clean. Next, I would put on an outfit I had stolen. I always stole name brands, like Versace, Gucci, and Fendi. Mom always taught me, if you don't have money, always keep yourself up and looking nice as much as possible. So I always ironed these outfits in the room before I put them on. People don't like to deal with broke people, she always said. I kept myself looking like I was stable, so I could eventually get something from somebody.

I ended up meeting a college student who had her

own place in the Five Points area of Atlanta. We got high all of the time on cocaine. When I moved out a short time later, I had no place to lay my head and nothing to eat, but I had something that was even more important to me: a drug habit.

I sold incense, doo-rags, and picture frames, all of which I had stolen. Some guys hustling around the Underground Mall tried to sell me some Coogi sweaters. The tags on them read around $500. I wanted to buy some, because the prices the people were asking seemed like a great deal. But a guy pulled me aside and told me they were getting those sweaters from a flea market, and they were not real. I was confident I could resell them at a profit, so I went to the flea market, bought some, and began to hustle them on the street out of a suitcase and a garbage bag.

I eventually started saving some money, but I spent it on ecstasy pills. I went to clubs every chance I got in order to stay warm, get away from the dangerous streets, and sell any pills I had left over. I ended up holding onto a few dollars every now and then and living in an apartment with another female. One day I woke up to find that she had used most of my coke. I choked her on the couch in that apartment and only stopped when the police came. Fortunately, she did not die, and I didn't go to jail, but that's when I found out that I really had a problem with cocaine.

So, it was back to the concrete jungle, as I called it, sleeping on the Marta, in the Greyhound bus station, at clubs, or wherever. I grabbed food anywhere I could, even at a shelter. All I did was pop pills, use cocaine, and smoke weed. I was exhausted and felt like my heart was going to give out on me. On a guy's advice, I went to the pharmacy at a K-mart in East Point and found out that I had the symptoms of a heart attack. Using a fake name, I told this young lady who worked there that I had been getting high on cocaine and was barely sleeping. I told her everything I thought she needed to know, so she could tell the EMT when they came. My heart was pumping, and I was feeling weak sitting in the chair, so I lay down on the floor.

Her supervisor came over and began yelling at me, all hysterical like. I was too weak to answer, and she wouldn't answer for me as we had planned. This supervisor's attitude made me so mad that I found enough strength to shove a chair at him, which made my blood pressure rise. Just then the paramedics showed up, put me on the stretcher , and carried me out the door and into the ambulance.

In the ambulance, I didn't take my eyes off the monitor. I knew if the line went flat, I would be dead. But watching the monitor was a crazy thing to do, because if it went flat, I wouldn't be around to know it. The EMT told me that I was okay and to leave the cocaine alone, because that was what was making my heart beat fast. When the police officer came on the ambulance, I gave him a fake I.D., which he detected and put me in cuffs. He said if the store manager said it was okay, he would let me go. But the manager said no, because he was still upset about my shoving the chair at him.

I ended up getting out of jail the same night, went to the bus station, and got on a bus to Jackson. I was just going to stop and say hello to my mom on my way to New Orleans. The Super Bowl and Mardi-Gras were about to occur, and I liked to follow the crowds and hustle where events were happening.

CHAPTER 12

Home Sweet Home

WHEN I ARRIVED back in Jackson, I got a ride to my cousin's dope house. I called a friend I had known most of my life and asked him to take me to Ma's house. When he came to pick me up, I noticed that his arm was in a sling. He said he had been shot with an AK- 47 assault rifle after leaving a club the weekend before. As we got about half-way to Ma's house, the truck made a loud "poof" sound. He said it had broken down, so we had to leave it in the middle of a busy boulevard. Getting out of the truck, I recognized a vehicle across the street. It belonged to the guys who I knew wanted revenge on me for taking their drugs without paying for them months before.

With no weapon to defend myself, I had to run into the closest store. It was empty, except for three older men talking to each other. "They're trying to kill me!" I yelled. As I was hiding my sandwich bag of pills under a shelf, I happened to notice what looked like a 6" chrome 44 magnum revolver on the counter. One of the guys said, "You did sometime wrong, and now you're scared!"

Just then my friend who had been driving me in the truck came in the store, and I put two and two together. I said, "Why did you set me up?" He said, "You tripping. Ain't nobody outside." I patted him down, looking for a gun, but found none. Less than a minute later I saw this guy who looked somewhat familiar on the other side of the store window. He pointed his finger at me and yelled, "We gonna get you, Montez!"

The police walked in the door a few moments later and arrested me for having a felony warrant. I was somewhat relieved, because I was sure the guy on the other side of the window had been hired to kill me.

Soon I was back in the Hinds County Jail, held without bond. That's the same jail where I'd had trouble with the gang. My first week in jail, I had a run-in with a guy I had met once when I was a teenager. He already had been sentenced to twenty-five years in federal court and was a very well-known drug dealer. When he told me to shut up while I was yelling out the cell door to someone upstairs, we had hostile words back and forth. He stood over six feet tall and weighed between 200 and 250 pounds. At the time I weighed about 140. Cocaine had caused me to lose a lot of weight, and my nose was constantly running and sometimes bleeding.

My cellmate told me that while he was out receiving medicine, he had overheard some guys in my cell block talking about jumping me. When the nurse left after giving out medication, I was already prepared to fight. My cellmate was right. One of the guards opened up our cell from the control panel, and the guy who had been talking about me ran in and locked the door behind him.

We hit each other with our fists and wrestled. I spit, kicked, and scratched at him until the officer who had let him in opened the door to stop the fight. As he pulled us off each other, I struck again. Word got to me that this guy's friends were going to get me. Since you can't run or have a gun in jail, I maneuvered the system by going to medical. After I left medical, they placed me on protective custody to keep me away from other inmates who were in population.

I was placed with a guy who was an enemy of the guy who fought me in my cell. He had been placed on administrative protective custody, because he had influence and the authorities were concerned that he might provoke a riot. He let me use his cell phone at night and gave me marijuana, food from restaurants, home-cooked food, cigarettes, and liquor. Plus, he kept the officer from locking my cell door at night. When he went to federal court and got his time, I really missed those things.

I signed off of protective custody, and they sent me, of all places, to the cell block where the guy I had fought was. Before long, five or six of his friends picked a fight over the cigarettes someone had smuggled in for me. I swung first, hoping I could at least take out one of them, and we fell to the floor. Some other inmates broke up the fight, and the guys all left the cell. There was no safety in jail. Around that time I got word that my cousin C.J. had just been stabbed in prison in Greene County. They rushed him to the hospital in a helicopter.

After thirteen rough months in the county jail, I finally went to court, where I saw Ma for the first time in a very long time. She looked good in her pinstripe suit. The judge gave me four years, so I went to prison for my second time. I was twenty-three years old.

CHAPTER 13

Prison to Prison to Prison

NOT LONG AFTER I arrived at the prison, I ran into a drug dealer I knew personally. He had the officers reassign his bunk partner so I could sleep on his top bunk. We smoked marijuana, took pictures with cameras, drank liquor, and even ate steak and shrimp. I had never been in a Mississippi prison that had cable television, but we did. We even watched videos. Prison is never comfortable, but this was the absolute best someone could do!

It turned out that the guy who tried to set me up to be killed about three years before was in this prison. He was the one who came to my hotel room and kept moving his gun closer to himself when I came near it. I talked to the officer I knew and had him moved into my dorm. Jesus said to love your enemies, so I treated him like a brother. The two of us had no problems after that.

At this facility, I also met a Vietnamese guy. He and I got close, and he sent me $1,000 after he was transferred out of our prison to another one. We planned to do big business together in the street when we had served our time.

After three years and nine months, I was released to go home. I was on extensive probation, but I immediately went back to the streets. I wanted to hook up with the Vietnamese guy I had met in prison, so while I was waiting for him to be released from federal prison, I went to stay with his brother. We stayed in a hotel that his relatives owned on Mississippi's Gulf Coast. Not long afterwards, I landed back in prison for the third time.

They sent me to the worst prison this time, the Mississippi State Penitentiary in Parchman. For years I had been hearing stories about the stabbings and even a killing there. The cellmate I was put with had been in there for fifteen years and was gang affiliated. It took him only fifteen minutes to make this clear.

I learned that if you weren't in the Black Gangster Disciples (B.G.D.) gang, you couldn't stand with them in line going to eat, recreation, etc. The same went for the Vice Lord (V.L.) gang. The other convicts who weren't in these gangs, which included me, had to stand directly between these two lines, or we'd get "dealt with," which meant "smashed," beat up, or stabbed. They called us neutral ones the "peons."

I happened to meet a guy who had a cousin who was my cousin. He was affiliated with a gang, and he insisted on giving me security from his fellow gang members. Normally prisoners go to the shower with their boots on because of the danger of assault. He and his gang buddies escorted me to the shower while I was wearing my shower shoes, waited until I came out, and walked me back to my cell. After I had been there only a short time, I was told one morning that I was being transferred to Greene County Prison. I was glad to get out of Parchman, because rumors were flying that a gang bang was going to take place when the cell doors opened only hours later.

Greene County Prison was where my cousin had been stabbed and almost killed. Officers made us do everything by the book; there was no slack. I didn't mind the strict rules, though, because it was safer. A while later I was transferred to another prison in Mississippi, which had more freedom and better food than the previous two. But after five weeks, I wanted to get closer to home, where I thought I could get marijuana to sell. My intention was to earn some money so I'd have some when I got out. I pretended to be mentally ill, and they sent me to Rankin County Prison in Pearl, Mississippi, where I was fifteen to twenty minutes away from home.

CHAPTER 14

Close and Yet So Far

ONCE IN RANKIN County Prison, I tried to find an officer who would smuggle drugs in for me, so I could sell them to convicts. But that didn't work, because gang members already had that business locked in.

Not long after I arrived, I was walking out of the chow hall with another inmate, who also was from Jackson, Mississippi, and we heard a guy say to his buddies, "Who them NIGGAS thank they is?" I suspect these guys had been watching us for some time, and I just kept on walking and pretended I didn't hear. Sometimes, especially in prison, it's best to ignore certain things. But the fellow from my home town, my homeboy, answered with his name, and they told him to come over. He went over and talked with them for a couple of minutes, and we left. I figured they just wanted to know who we were, because I had been trying to find a connection to market marijuana in the prison.

My homeboy was a gang affiliate, but he was "laid back," which means he wasn't active. But because I was not affiliated at all, it seemed I was prey everywhere. When we got back to our housing unit, we were hanging around on the racks (beds), and I noticed two or three heads peeking in. They looked like they might be up to no good, but when I told my homeboy, he sloughed it off. I persisted, so he said he would talk to the OG (Original Gangster) to calm the tension, if there was any. I was so nervous that I had to use the stool (toilet), which I did with one leg out my pants in case I needed to fight or run. That's the way convicts there used the stool, because something could go down anytime.

Later, as I lay down for the night, I kept my boots on. We were in an open dorm with about 120 beds for convicts. A guy I didn't know, who had big muscles and tattoos, including on his face, tapped me and said with curses, "What was that stuff you said to my brother?" He meant his brother in the gang.

I pretended I didn't know he even had a brother. Then I glanced over and saw someone else at the end of my bed standing directly over me. Another convict with rippling muscles that appeared to be covered with baby oil was standing down by the officer's guard tower, but no attention was being paid to me when I needed it most. Sensing something was wrong, I made the first move and grabbed the guy with the tattooed face. I don't know what happened after that. All I can remember is that I ran as hard as I had ever run in my life toward the door. It was normally locked, but that night, miraculously, it was open.

I was escorted to the medical station, and the lieutenant automatically put me in protective custody. I left with a patch on my eye and patches on my side to stop the bleeding. I don't know what caused the cuts, maybe a knife, but I was too busy getting away to see anything.

After that incident, I was put in a one-man cell, and they only let me out about three hours a week to make phone calls and take a shower. Before I was let out, I had to place my wrists through a hole in the cell bars to get handcuffed. Once out of the cell, my feet were shackled. This happened every time I left the cell, except for showers. When I went to the recreation yard, I had to stay in a cage. I could only see the sky through the top of the cage. I never saw grass. That sure taught me to appreciate God's earth.

I met a guy in the cell next to me who had escaped from jail with a gun and shot a police officer. I wanted to witness to him, because he was dying of cancer, but I couldn't because I was so trapped in sin myself.

While I was in prison, I also met Edgar Ray Killen. He had been involved in a plot that resulted in the death of two civil rights supporters. Some guys said he also had plotted to kill Dr. Martin Luther King, Jr., but that wasn't true. I recently found out that the movie *Mississippi Burning* is based on this man's crime. Even though some people in the prison disapproved, I "cooked" his noodles for him. That's what we called it when we flushed the toilet many, many times to get the water as hot as possible. Then we'd put the warm water on noodles. I prepared meals for Mr. Edgar Ray this way. He was in a wheel chair and very old. Sometimes he would tell me that his wife or someone else he knew said for him to thank me for helping him out.

I stayed busy, even in a cell by myself. I made business plans about the money and merchandise I hoped to get when I got out. I counted bricks and did a lot of other stuff that amounted to nothing, but I never sought after God. It got to the point to where I would attend Ju'mar at Muslim meetings; I would do this instead of serving Jehovah. I was aware that I was on the wrong path, but I ignored my conscience.

CHAPTER 15

Rotten Big Apple

MY SENTENCE WAS up on a Sunday, after I had served one year. Ma and the family picked me up and headed straight from prison to church. Even though I was in church, and even though deep down inside I wanted to be delivered from the things of this world, I was mired too deep.

God had told me not to get back involved with pimping when I was released, so I only did it occasionally. In prison I had the desire to settle down with one female, something I had never done. So I married, but it didn't last. She stayed gone too long one night, and I changed the lock. That was our last day together. No one knew we had married until later, when it was all over. I married not really having a good understanding of what marriage was about. It was my attempt to do the right thing by having one woman in my life. I wanted to see what it felt like to come home after work, pay the bills as a husband,

and be one lady's man. I was tired of the streets.

After a few months, I got a job at a Saturn car dealership. I was enjoying working, and I was staying out of the streets. All I did was work every day and save as much as I could to get some clothes and shoes that I could sell. I was living the plan I had thought about night and day while in prison. Usually, I would have been already in the streets hustling to get money, so I felt good working a job and trying to stay straight. It was illegal to sell fake shoes and clothes, but to me it was more legit than robbing, stealing, or selling some kind of dope.

I saved about four or five whole paychecks and bought a roundtrip Greyhound bus ticket to New York City. After a thirty-two-hour bus ride up, I bought some merchandise to sell, sent most back to Jackson via UPS, and loaded the most expensive item, a box of shoes, on the bus. I still planned to keep my job at the dealership, but I was excited about the prospect of making a few dollars selling merchandise, so I wouldn't have to rely just on my paycheck. For the first time in my life, I was really enjoying working.

On the way back from New York, we made plenty of stops. I checked the luggage compartment under the bus from time to time to make sure my shoes were safe. When we arrived in Jackson, I eagerly waited for my box of shoes to be unloaded, but it wasn't there. The last time

I remember seeing it was in Birmingham, Alabama. I was sick! I thought of all the time and money I had spent to make the trip up to New York City and back, and all the effort it took to buy those shoes and lug them around the city. Now they had been stolen! What a mess. I already had people lined up to purchase these goods, and I had counted on making far more money than I had spent.

It didn't take long for me to make other plans. Not long after, I left my job and went to Houston, Texas. I was still on probation, but I lied to my probation officer about having a job there. I was hoping to find a drug connection where I could get dope a lot cheaper than in Jackson, so I could make a bigger profit.

After I got to Houston, I did get a job, but I only stayed there for about nine months before heading back to Mississippi. I had collected quite a large amount of shoes to sell, and I had established a drug connection on marijuana. I thought I was stable, but really I was drunk on false dreams.

Back home, I overheard somebody I knew on the phone say angrily that no one had gotten her boyfriend out of jail yet, so I put up the bond. That gave me favor with this guy I had bonded out and with his buddies, who were passionate about living by the gun. That night I gave one of them a small bag of cocaine; the next day I offered the same guy a pound of marijuana. We became friends, and I made plans for us to do business together.

Seemed like every day back home I relaxed by "sipping syrup," which is codeine and methamphetamine mixed in a soda pop; or I would pop ecstasy pills and smoke "purple," which is high-grade marijuana. I hadn't taken any cocaine since that heart-racing experience in the ambulance in Atlanta, but I did hustle it, along with marijuana and shoes.

CHAPTER 16

No Joy Ride

ONE AFTERNOON I was riding in the car with a friend I had been staying with. We were going to pick up her friend's child from school. Approaching the school, there were barriers in the road, so we had to make a U-turn. As we did, we found ourselves directly facing another car; the headlights of our two cars were only about ten feet apart.

At that moment a guy I had seen just a couple of times before got out of the back seat of the other car. He was carrying two handguns, one in each hand. They looked like Glock 40 and Glock 45 automatics. Suddenly, he pointed them at our windshield and started firing. I dove down on the floor, hands over my head. I realized that we needed to get out of our car because that guy might be coming our way. I grabbed my friend's hand to try to get her to come with me, but she jerked it back. So I opened the passenger door and made a dash for it.

APPREHENDED *for* LIFE

That was a dangerous move, with bullets flying at close range, and I felt bad about leaving my friend in the car, but there wasn't much else I could do. I ran in between some houses and stayed there until the shooting stopped.

When I saw that the guy and his friends had gone, I went back to the car. The windshield was full of holes. One of the bullets had pierced the headrest on the driver's seat, so my friend would have been killed if she hadn't ducked. Thank God, she was still alive.

She drove us back to her place, where I had been staying. The same guys must have come to the house, because there were bullet holes where I usually laid my head to sleep. There were also bullet holes in the front window, the couch, and the walls in the bathroom and the dining room.

Every day after that I couldn't hustle anymore out in public because of the danger, so I began to lose money. I kept a chrome semi-automatic assault rifle on the back seat of the car everywhere I went. I was paranoid and alert for anything. I even had people sneak a gun into clubs for me. It was very uncomfortable trying to run from God. He was calling me the whole time. Years later, after I made peace with God, I even made peace with some of those guys who had been shooting at us.

For three months I mostly stayed inside, out of sight.

I had no money and was depressed. Then, all of a sudden, I started making an average of $5,000 per day hustling illegally. In one week, I financed a used luxury truck and a car that was almost new. I bought a new wardrobe, supplied my expensive drug habit, partied hard at clubs, and fulfilled lots of the fleshly desires I had been postponing. Now that the money I had been chasing for a long time was flowing in, I really thought I was having fun.

I ended up getting married again, this time to the girl who had driven the car that was in the shooting at the school. I was thinking that this was the best way to stop committing adultery. I didn't tell Ma. I knew what I was supposed to be doing; I just didn't do it. Within months after the marriage, we were separated, and eventually we divorced.

Even my drug connection in Texas fell apart; apparently someone told my contact that I was plotting to harm him, which was a lie that could have gotten me killed. Around the same time, my little ten-year-old cousin Javaris (Aunt Mary's son) was shot in the head and died, and my dad's brother, Uncle Shark, died.

At this time I was on probation, and I wasn't supposed to go to any clubs, but I went one night anyway. As I was leaving, there was a man lying on the ground in the parking lot. He'd been shot. A lot of people were gathered around him; they were saying he was dead, but he wasn't.

This sounds weird, but as lost as I was, I stood over him and prayed that he would be fine. I even followed the ambulance to the hospital and prayed for him there. I had been at the hospital only about fifteen minutes when a cop came over to me and asked if I had been at the club. I lied, because I could have been sent to prison for violating parole. The cop told me that if they found out I had been at the club, I'd be charged for murder. But he lied because I heard a few months later that the guy who had been shot was still alive, but in ICU.

CHAPTER 17

Hustling

GOD WAS ON me hard. I had no peace; I was para-noid. Even the money that once made me feel so secure vanished. Less than nine months from the time money was flowing in and life seemed to be getting better, I was separated and out on my own with no vehicle and no place to live. I was staying in shotgun hotels, as I call them, and was barely making it day by day. My clothes and shoes had been stolen. I had no merchandise to sell and no money to buy more. It was crazy.

I tried hustling again, but almost immediately I got busted and went to jail. When I was released, I knew I couldn't continue like this. I felt I had to find a way to save money and better myself. I was thinking that in physical terms, not spiritual.

I heard about a job in Brunswick, Georgia, that would let me be a salesman door to door, so I went to the barber in Jackson and got the locks cut out my head, for a fresh new start. Chauncey dropped me off at the train station, and I took the train to Atlanta. From Atlanta, I caught a bus to Brunswick.

The job was selling magazine subscriptions door-to-door for this small business. We crisscrossed Florida, Georgia, and North and South Carolina. After a few weeks, though, I began to get suspicious that this company was a scam. I had the feeling that the people I worked for were simply keeping people's money and had no intention of fulfilling the magazine subscriptions.

I decided that if I was going to hustle, I'd do it for myself. So I got together a portfolio with the list of magazines and other sales literature and started going door to door in Georgia on my own. During this period I met a woman in a club. We started living together, and in less than a year she was pregnant.

Not long after I got to Brunswick, the Lord removed the compulsion to get rich. I felt convicted in my spirit about making money illegally. For my whole life I'd tried to get rid of that compulsion, but I'd always failed. It was good to finally be free, but my change in character really hurt my cash flow. I didn't have the same drive. I could hustle only enough to pay bills when they came due.

One day, when I was selling these bogus magazines in Savannah, Georgia, I was under even more pressure than normal to make some money. I had to get back to Brunswick that night by 5:00 p.m. and pay my light bill, or our electricity would be shut off. When I rang the bell on a house in a nice neighborhood, a woman opened the door. After we had talked for a while, she invited me in. She said she didn't want any magazines. Then she put $20 in my hand. I thanked her, but I needed more money to pay my electric bill, so I still tried to sell her magazines.

She said she didn't want any magazines, and she just started talking about the Lord. She went on and on about the Lord. In my head a voice was saying, "Tell her these magazines aren't real. Tell her you're a fake." I was fighting so hard against this voice. The last thing I wanted to do was confess to her that I was trying to con her, especially in her home.

Finally, it got to be too much. I broke down and said, "I've got to tell you something; these magazines are fake." It was sure hard to tell her the truth, but I couldn't help myself. I tried to give the money back to her, even though I really needed it, but she wouldn't take it. She said, "I knew you weren't telling the truth; you're not a good liar."

Then she started to pray for me. Her husband came out of the back of the house and prayed with us. I was crying and asking God's forgiveness. She told me to praise God, so I was saying, "Hallelujah, Hallelujah." She put her hand on my stomach and told me, "Praise him louder! Really get it out!"

I started shouting, "HALLELUJAH! HALLE-LUJAH!" All of a sudden, I felt a tremendous relief, like a burden had rolled off of me. It felt so good! I felt cleaner and freer than I had in a long time.

The woman's name was Mrs. Ranch. She told me to get rid of that portfolio of magazine stuff—the price lists and everything—and to quit hustling, or I'd wind up in jail or dead. She said that God was going to prosper me, and that I was going to have so much joy that I wouldn't be able to stop smiling. She said I was a leader, and that it was going to be a slow process, but that I would walk with God.

CHAPTER 18

Cell 316

THE DATE WAS January 6, 2010. I was still reeling from that time with Mrs. Ranch as I made the one-hour drive back to Brunswick. When I got home, I found out that someone had loaned us the money to pay our electric bill, with no strings attached. The bill was paid before 5:00 p.m.

I quit hustling and started looking very, very hard for a job. I filled out countless job applications, but my good intentions did not get me a job or stop the mailman from bringing the bills. I reached the breaking point and was praying and crying. We constantly faced eviction, but I remembered Mrs. Ranch's caution that I'd better not hustle, or I'd end up in jail or dead.

Finally, I asked God to have mercy on me, and I started hustling again. I felt really bad doing it, but I figured God would forgive me. At least I hoped he would. The Holy Spirit was really convicting me, but I didn't fully listen, because I was still blind in sin. God had better plans for me, though, and he didn't waste any time. Within three days I was in jail.

I went to jail on April 6, exactly three months after that encounter with Mrs. Ranch. I was feeling especially bad, because my girlfriend was due to give birth in just a few months, while I'd still be in jail. Even more than that, the words of Mrs. Ranch were still playing in my ear.

In jail, I did nothing but worry. I was worried about how my girlfriend, who had no job and was pregnant, would make it with the bills and eviction notices. I was worried about being sent to prison; I was worried about whether I would get bonded out; I was worried about lots of things, big and small. I worried, worried, worried.

I was "bucking," which means I was fighting against the things of God. I walked in circles all the time, thinking about the walls of Jericho. Later, I began communicating with a guy who told me that he once was a minister, but he fell. We talked a lot, and he helped me more than words can describe. I hate to say this, but I was glad he was in jail. I thanked God for sending me this angel.

This man explained scriptures to me that opened my eyes up again, and he answered questions that I needed to know. His lovely wife, a true soldier for Christ, stuck by his side. She helped us by sending Bible literature copied from books, and even bought books for us to study. It was fun and took the stress off of us. We sat at the table everyday, filling ourselves with the knowledge of God. We kept some kind of Bible literature on the table, from early morning until lockdown at night.

I found out from my public defender that I may be looking at twenty years when my record came from Mississippi. I went to praying hard and seeking the face of the Lord. Every time I got close to bonding out, something seemed to block it. God was letting me exhaust all my options, to show me that he was the only one who could save me. I know now that God deserves all the glory. I learned that from the training and purging I received in those cell walls.

We prayed together, fasted together, and witnessed to others as well. We wrote songs and sung them. We did everything in the name of the Lord. Another angel named Mrs. Kathy Roberts came to church services on Sunday. She answered all of our questions and even sent us letters with scriptures we really needed. Sister Kathy is so faithful in serving the word of God to the inmates. She made us all feel so special as she gave her love to a dying generation.

I was in cell 316, which caused me to think about John 3:16: "For God so loved the world that he gave his one and only son, that whosoever believes in him will not perish, but will have eternal life." I often would put a sheet over my cell window so I could pray in private. I prayed that the good Lord would draw my girlfriend to him, help her out on paying bills, send godly friends to her, and that one day we would get married, whether I was in jail or not. She had just given birth to my only biological child, Sirius Montez Terrell Alford, and I prayed that I would get out and raise him to become a powerful man of God. I begin to feel selfish praying for my own life so much, so I started praying for everyone else except me. Then the good Lord told me one day to just praise Him, so I started offering more praise and fewer petitions.

God started to move in my life even more. I remember I was sleeping one day, and I was literally awakened while I was asleep. I saw Ma and my sister behind me at what looked like a counter. I turned toward them and said, "Praise God! Praise God!" While I was experiencing this supernatural experience, my mouth was opening as if I was speaking naturally, but I could not hear myself.

Then I saw some rows of folding chairs on the right, left, and in front of me. They all had purple banners on their backrests with scriptures written in gold, which I couldn't read. There was a dark-skinned guy in one of the chairs on my left, who had no hair on his head at all. He had his head down the whole time, as if he was asleep or praying.

In one of the chairs in front of me was a man whose head was shining bright like the sun in the summer, except the color of the light was white instead of yellow. As I looked upon him, my eyes were not blinded by the brightness. He was sitting down with what looked like a portfolio and some books in his lap. I only saw him for less than one second.

By this time I was on my knees with my hands up in the air praising God. A thought entered my head that I was actually communicating with God. I wasn't hearing his actual voice, just reading His thoughts. He read mine as well.

I thought of freedom, and I felt in my spirit that was not what God wanted me to think about. Then I saw a picture of the faces of my girlfriend and son, but again I felt in my spirit that wasn't what I was meant to focus on. Next, I thought of how King Solomon pleased God by asking for wisdom, so I asked God for wisdom, and the same thought entered my mind that I was still missing what he wanted. Finally, it seemed that he commanded my spirit to lie down with the side of my face on the floor and glorify and worship him.

As I did that, a feeling that can only come from God came over me. The same face I had seen that shined bright like a white sun was in my stomach. My entire body felt so warm and so good that I can't describe it. It was way better than sex or anything else you could imagine on earth. I don't know how long that feeling lasted, maybe less than a second, but I do know that there was a whole lot of joy in me.

I opened my eyes and went straight to the word of God. I opened the Bible randomly, and my eyes landed on Psalm 21: "Oh Lord, the king rejoices in your strength. How great is his joy in the victories you give!" That psalm seemed to describe exactly what I was experiencing—being in the presence of God and blessed with his goodness.

CHAPTER 19

Free

AS MY COURT date drew near, I fasted, prayed, sang hymns, and meditated on the twentieth chapter of Second Chronicles, which talks about how the battle is the Lord's. I was ready for whatever sentence I would be given, knowing that God, not man, determines my fate. If I got five to seven years, I wouldn't complain. I figured they wouldn't let me off easy, because of my previous convictions. I had already planned that if I had to go back to prison, I was going to study the Word day and night until I came home.

In court, when I was asked about my charges, I testified about my life being changed by God while I was in jail. They released me that day, December 15, 2010. I walked out of jail praising God and happy, happy, happy!

I didn't have much concern about how I was going to get home; I was just so overwhelmed in the grace of God. A little while later, I called to tell my family how God had opened doors for me. Mom was excited after

I called her. My girlfriend, who was now the mother of my son, arranged for one of her friends to pick me up at a McDonald's, a few miles from the jail.

When I got home to my girlfriend, I told her I loved her and that I wanted the two of us to get married. I was on fire for God, and it wasn't right for us to be living together unmarried. God seemed to be answering my prayers, because she had been going to church, which was a miracle considering the way we had thought and acted before I went to jail. My prayer day and night was to marry the woman that I loved and do the work of the Lord.

It was hard to find a job, too. But this time I always looked to God for our finances, and he never failed me. I had a vision in my sleep that I was going to have a job at a food place. In the vision, there were two fryers, like the ones at McDonalds. There was a manager who got blessed for hiring me, and another Christian on the job. So I started applying to every food place I could think of, mostly as a cook. But there were no openings, so I enrolled in Le Cordon Bleu Culinary Arts School in Orlando, Florida, but I withdrew after a while because I sensed that wasn't God's plan.

It was very hard finding that job that I saw in the vision, so I took a job landscaping. When that work slowed down, I remembered that I had applied to King and

Prince Seafood, which is a respected national company headquartered in Brunswick. I called them back on my birthday, the second of August, and they hired me. I started orientation three days later. Not long after I started at King and Prince, they made a deal to supply frozen fish to McDonalds. The vision I had was coming to pass; the Lord Almighty had grace enough to reveal to me what he was going to do. I've had that job for eight months now, and I've never been happier at any job in my life. Recently I got a promotion.

The company gives its employees discounts on its products, so one day I bought some frozen fish. It was too much to put in our refrigerator, so I got on my bike and gave some away to the first person the Lord directed me to. It made me happy to be able to help someone, and I was ready to give more.

About five days later, I was talking to the human resource director about donating food to churches. God opened the door for us to give 4,470 pounds of seafood to some inner-city ministries. The company is prospering, and I believe it's because they are remembering the poor.

In December 2011, my mom made the long trip from Jackson to visit us and the kids Sirius, December and Star. She also witnessed me marry Lakisha Kenea Alford. It was so good to see her again and to tell her how the

Lord has saved me, in answer to all her prayers over the years. She blessed us so much with her love of God and knowledge of the Word. I've started college part time, and I now have a car.

In March 2011, I went back to Savannah to thank Mrs. Ranch, the prophet of the Lord who had prayed for me with her husband. On the one-hour drive from Brunswick, I was wishing I had a gospel CD so I could listen to Christian music.

When Mrs. Ranch came to the door, I asked her if she remembered me. She said, "Oh, yes, you're the minister." I told her she must have me confused with someone else, because I wasn't a minister. She said, "I know exactly who you are; God told me you're a minister. " We talked for a while. I thanked her for playing such an important role in my life and told her how God had truly prospered me, just as she had said. She said she was glad to see I was walking with the Lord and some other encouraging things. Then, before I left, she brought something out from the back room, placed it on the table, and said, "The Lord told me to give you this." It was a gospel CD.

CHAPTER 20

Thankful

THAT'S MY STORY, so far at least. As you can see, I haven't been walking with the Lord very long, so you may be wondering why I'm writing this book. After all, I'm still young, although I'm a lot older than I deserve to be. I could've been killed many times before now.

In the seventeenth chapter of Luke, it says that ten men who had leprosy came to Jesus and asked to be healed. Jesus told them to go and show themselves to the priest. They obeyed, and on the way they were healed. However, only one of the ten came back to give thanks and praise. Jesus said, "Were not all ten healed. Where are the other nine?"

I'm writing this book because I don't want to be like the nine ungrateful lepers. I want to be like the one who came back to thank Jesus. I want to give God the glory for setting me free and saving my life, physically and spiritually.

The fifth chapter of Mark tells about a man who was possessed by so many demons that they were called

Legion. Jesus cast the demons out of the man and set him completely free. The man followed Jesus, but Jesus told him to go home and tell people about the great and marvelous things the Lord had done for him.

I feel like that man, too. Jesus has delivered me from a whole lot of demons: drugs, lust, craving for money, anger, and a bunch more. Like that man, I want to glorify Jesus. I want to tell people what marvelous things God has done for me.

I know God's will for me. God released me from jail so I can praise him and do some work for him. That's why I'm so passionate. I know my purpose.

I'm not bitter about the bad things that have happened to me, because I can see the purpose for them. His word says that "all things work together for good, for them that love God, who are called according to his purpose." Now that I'm working in my purpose, I'm not anxious. I have peace. There's a lot of stuff going on in my life, but I'm not worried about any of it. He took away all the worrying and replaced it with joy. Like it says in the Bible, the joy of the Lord is my strength. I'm happy, happy, happy!

Now I understand that all the negative stuff I've been through was preparing me for the work I have to do. It was making me into the man I am today. Even the bad things other people did to me and I did to myself now are working for good. I was weak, but these trials made me strong in Christ.

All of that bad stuff makes me love God even more. I want to tell other people even more about how good God is. Because of what I've been through, I can understand people who are in the same kind of situations.

I've still got plenty of challenges in my life, but they seem petty to me compared to what I've experienced. They're nothing compared to the power and goodness of God. I want to praise Jesus every way I can. He apprehended me, and I'm so glad he did. No more running away from anything. I surrendered, and he filled me with unspeakable joy.

That's why I'm writing this book. I want you to know him, too.

My frienD Grayson I
wrote this book to thank my
Mom for teaching me what's right.
I never listened and stayed
in alot of trouBle. I want
you to make better choices than
I did. Listen to your mom
and grandmom, dad & everyone's
teaching. Peace Be gooD ☺